SABRINA FISHER REECE

Staying Happy in the Midst of Havoc

How to Hold on to Joy and Peace When the World is Falling Apart

First published by In59Seconds Publishing 2026

First edition

This book was professionally typeset on Reedsy.
Find out more at reedsy.com

This book is dedicated to the person who is holding it together on the outside while everything inside feels heavy, uncertain, or quietly overwhelming. It is for the one who keeps showing up for their family, their responsibilities, and their life, even when fear tries to take over. This book is for the one who is searching for peace, not because life is easy, but because life has demanded more strength than they ever expected to give. Don't Give up! Happiness is a Choice..

-Bri Reece

Contents

Introduction

There are moments in life that arrive without warning and change the way you see everything. You wake up expecting a normal day, and within a single phone call, a single headline, or a health diagnosis, everything shifts. One minute you are grounded and happy, and the next you are trying to steady yourself while the world feels uncertain, unpredictable, and sometimes even frightening.

We are living in a time where uncertainty is not occasional. It seems to be constant at times. You turn on the news and hear about conflict, war, and decisions being made that affect millions of people who had no say in them. You scroll through your phone and see stories that remind you how fragile life can be. You hear about families losing their homes to fire, people fighting systems they trusted, and situations that make you stop and ask how any of it is fair. These are not distant realities anymore. These things are happening to us or people close to us regularly. They are part of the world we wake up in every single day.

At the same time, life continues to happen on a personal level. A parent receives a phone call that their child has been hurt. A grandparent watches a moment unfold that could have ended very differently. A mother sits with information about her own health that forces her to confront fear in a way she never imagined. A husband loses the job he was planning to retire with and he is responsible for the mortgage.

These are the kinds of moments that test not just your strength, but your ability to stay present, to stay grounded, and to stay emotionally steady when everything inside you wants to scream.

It would be easy to let all of this take over. It is perfectly understandable to fall into fear, to feel overwhelmed, or to carry a constant sense of anxiety about what might happen to you or your family next. Many people do, and there is no judgment in that. The weight of the world combined with personal challenges can feel like too much for anyone to carry. The problem is that when fear takes over, it does not just sit subtly in the distant background. It begins to shape your thoughts, your emotions, your reactions. Fear prevents you from experiencing any sense of peace.

This book was not written from a place of theory. It was written from lived experience. I have been there personally and felt everything I am writing about. This book comes from moments that could have easily led to panic and fear taking full control, moments where the outcome was terribly uncertain, and moments where maintaining peace required intention, discipline, and a conscious decision not to be consumed by what was happening at the moment. Which is not easy to do, I must say.

There have been situations that could have shaken my faith to the core. I have had moments that could have caused everything I owned to spiral downward. I have had many experiences that demanded strength not just for survival, but for the people who depend on my strength.

What I have learned through all of it is something very simple, but not always easy to practice. There are many things in this world that are completely outside of our control, no matter how much we wish it were different. We cannot control global events, unexpected emergencies, or the actions of other people. We can't prevent every difficult moment from happening. What we can control, and what we must learn to protect, is how we respond.

The way you respond in any given moment has the power to shape your entire experience, determining whether what you are facing overwhelms you or whether you are able to move through it with clarity, intention, and emotional stability. There is always a point where a situation can either pull you under or be something you navigate through with awareness, and that point is found in how you choose to meet it internally. The internal discipline is the most important.

When fear begins to rise, it can feel immediate, urgent and all consuming, almost as if it is taking control without permission, yet there is still space within you to pause, take a breath and decide whether you will allow it to take over your thoughts or whether you will create room for something else to exist alongside it. That space inside of you is where you will find your peace, not in the absence of difficulty, because life will always bring challenges, but in your ability to remain grounded and calm even while difficulty is present. I am not saying this is always easy to do. My initial nature is to be impulsive. It is a learned behavior that requires continued cultivation until it becomes a way of life.

In the middle of everything that happens, it becomes very easy to lose yourself in the situation, to become fully absorbed in the emotions, the uncertainty, and the weight of what you are experiencing. At the same time, there is a deeper part of you that needs to remain steady so a solution can be found. That peaceful part of all of us does not have to disappear just because life feels overwhelming at the time. Staying connected to that calmer part of yourself is what allows you to move through life without losing your sense of who you are. No matter what unfolds around you. It gives you the opportunity to pause and decide what your next move is.

Choosing peace does not mean ignoring the reality of what is happening. It does not mean pretending that painful situations do not exist or that everything is fine when it is not. It means acknowledging what is happening without allowing it to take control of your emotional state. It means creating a level of awareness that allows you to step back, breathe, and decide how you are going to move forward instead of reacting from a place of fear, anger, disappointment or compulsion.

We can live in this world without being totally consumed by it. There is a way to experience difficult moments without allowing them to define your entire emotional state. Shifting you into fear, which can prevent you from thinking clearly. It is not easy but it is possible to remain present, grounded, and even hopeful while everything around you feels uncertain. That way is not something any of us are born with. It is something we build from the inside out, something we can practice, and something we can always return to again and again.

This book is here to guide you through that process. It is here to remind you that peace is not something you wait for when life decides to calm down. Peace is something you choose, protect, and remember to return to, even when the world is full of havoc. This book was written to help you understand that happiness is not a denial of reality. It isn't telling you to ignore your current situation. It is showing you how to make the decision to remain steady and calm within the ciaos, no matter what.

As you move through these pages, you will see real experiences, real life challenges, and real moments that required a conscious choice to stay grounded. You will also find practical ways to shift your mindset, protect your energy, and return to a place of joy and peace when everything feels overwhelming. This is not about perfection. It is about self mastery and awareness.

You are not expected to control the world around you. Nor are you expected to prevent every difficult moment from happening. No one expects you to carry everything without feeling anything. What you are capable of doing is learning how to hold on to your peace, how to protect your emotional well-being, and how to choose your response in a way that supports your life instead of taking away from it.

No matter what is happening around you, there is still a space within you that can remain stable and steady. There is still a place where peace can exist. This book will help you find it, strengthen it, and return to it whenever you need to.

One

When the World Feels Out of Control

Sometimes there comes a point in life when you realize that no matter how responsible you are, no matter how informed you try to be, and no matter how much you care about doing the right thing, there are forces in this world that operate far beyond your reach. You can wake up, go to work, take care of your family, vote, stay aware, and still find yourself living in a reality shaped by decisions you never made. That realization can feel unsettling because it challenges the belief that if you do everything right, life will respond in a way that feels safe and predictable.

Right now, we are living in a time where that illusion has been stripped away for many people and for many reasons. The idea that life will remain constant if you follow the rules no longer feels like a guaranteed certainty. We wake up to horrible news of war, conflict, and global tension, and that has a way of entering our space whether we invite it in or not. You might be going about your day, focused on your responsibilities, and suddenly you are faced with information that reminds you how fragile everything can be. It is not just something happening somewhere else anymore. It becomes something you feel, something that lingers in the back of your mind, something that quietly asks, what if this affects me next.

I remember a time when I was living in California and someone mentioned, very casually, that the state could one day break off and fall into the ocean due to seismic activity along the San Andreas Fault. That statement stayed with me longer than it should have, not because it was immediately believable, but because it planted a thought in my mind that I began to entertain. I found myself going online, researching and reading articles, trying to understand whether something like that was even possible, and even though the scientific reality is far more complex, with experts explaining that while California does experience earthquakes due to tectonic plate movement, the idea of the entire state suddenly dropping into the ocean is not how geology actually works, the thought had already done what thoughts often do when left unchecked. It created a sense of fear within me tied to something that was not actively happening and may never happen in that way at all.

Even with facts and statistics, even with logical explanations that showed that tectonic plates shift gradually over millions of years rather than collapsing overnight, there was still a moment where my mind held onto the possibility and turned it into something worth worrying about. I even caught myself thinking, hoping that if something like that were to happen, it would not happen before I had the chance to move. Looking back, that thought alone is a perfect example of how easily the mind can take an idea and run with it, no matter how unlikely or misunderstood, and turn it into a source of anxiety. The truth is, if something of that magnitude were ever to occur, it would not be something I could control, predict, or prevent, and living in fear of it would not change the outcome in any way.

That is how awareness, when it is not managed, can begin to shift the way you move through your life. It does not always come from real, immediate danger, but from the possibilities your mind begins to entertain and hold onto. You can become more anxious without realizing why, more guarded in situations that do not require it, and more consumed with outcomes that have not happened and may never happen. The mind starts to blur the line between what is real and what is imagined, between what is happening now and what could possible happen someday, and once that line becomes unclear, it becomes much harder to hold onto a sense of peace.

There is a difference between being informed and allowing every piece of information to take up space in your emotional world. When your mind is constantly scanning for what could go wrong, it begins to live in a future that does not exist, creating tension in the present moment that was never meant to be carried for that long. Thoughts begin to build on each other, scenarios begin to play out, and before you realize it, you are reacting to something that is not even happening. That is where the real work begins, in recognizing when your mind has gone beyond awareness and into unnecessary fear, and bringing yourself back to what is actually in front of you, to what is real, and to what you can truly respond to in that moment.

At the same time, life continues to unfold in very personal ways. You can be dealing with your own real challenges while also carrying the weight of what is happening in the world around you. A phone call from your child's school can instantly shift your entire emotional state. A moment of panic can take over before you even have time to process what is happening. You find yourself trying to stay calm, trying to think clearly, and trying to be strong for someone else while your own emotions are rising all at once. That experience alone is enough to overwhelm anyone, and yet it exists alongside everything else the world is already asking you to carry.

On March 23rd, 2026, I received a phone call from my daughter Journey's school telling me that she had been in an accident and was being transported to the hospital. Any parent understands that a call like that alone feels like it takes years off your life. In that moment, nothing else matters. Your heart drops, your thoughts begin to race, and all you want is to get to your child as quickly as possible.

When I arrived at the school, the ambulance was already there. Journey was only thirteen at the time and had never experienced anything like this before. She was trying to stay calm, but she was in a lot of pain. When she talked to me on phone before I got there, she immediately began to cry, and in that moment I knew that I could not fall apart. As much as it hurt me to see her like that, I had to be her calm. I had to be her strength.

It turned out that she and another child had been horse playing, and it resulted in her falling and dislocating her knee. Seeing your child in pain like that is something you cannot prepare for, and everything in you wants to react emotionally, to panic, and to let the fear take over. At the same time, I have trained myself to look for the brighter side, even in difficult moments. I had to remind myself that it could have been worse. Her leg could have been broken. It could have been something far more serious.

Right there in that moment, I made a conscious shift into gratitude. I focused on the fact that although she was hurt, this was something that could heal. She is young, her body is strong, and with time and rehabilitation, she would recover. We spent several hours at the hospital, and after extensive X-rays, the doctor was able to pop her knee back into place. We were able to go home and begin the healing process together.

Journey is my baby, my youngest child, and seeing her hurt naturally made me want to panic, but I understood that if I allowed myself to lose control emotionally, it would only make the situation harder for her. She needed to feel safe. She needed to feel supported. It was important that she saw that even though she was in pain, everything was going to be okay.

There is a unique kind of pressure that comes from living in both of these realities at the same time. On one side, there are global events that remind you how little control you truly have, situations unfolding in the world that can feel overwhelming and uncertain. On the other side, there are deeply personal moments like this, moments that require your full presence, your strength, and your ability to respond with clarity even when your emotions are rising. In those moments, it can feel like there is no space to pause, no time to process, and not one moment to simply exist without something demanding your attention or your emotional energy, yet it is within that exact pressure that you are reminded of your ability to choose your response, to ground yourself, and to show up in a way that brings calm into the chaos instead of adding to it.

Many people respond to this by becoming consumed with everything that is happening. They stay plugged into every update, every headline and current event, every piece of information in the news that confirms how uncertain things are. It can feel like staying informed is the responsible thing to do, and to a certain extent, it is. The problem begins when awareness turns into overload, and information turns into fear. At that point, you are no longer simply aware of what is happening. You are carrying it, internalizing it, and allowing it to shape how you feel throughout your day.

In my personal opinion, the news has a way of immediately pulling your attention into everything that is going wrong in the world, and when that becomes the first thing you take into your mind at the start of your day, it can quietly set the tone for everything that follows. It is not that staying informed is wrong, because there is value in knowing what is happening around you, but there is also wisdom in recognizing how and when you allow that information to enter your space. The reality is that most of what is presented is centered around conflict, loss, and negativity, and while those things exist, beginning your day with that energy can shift your emotional state before you have even had a moment to ground yourself.

There is a level of balance that has to be created in what you allow into your mind, especially in the morning when your thoughts are most impressionable and your emotional state is still being formed. That information on the news is not going anywhere. The headlines will still be there later, the updates will still be available, and the world will continue to move whether you check it immediately or not. What matters is how you choose to begin your day, because that beginning has the power to influence how you think, how you feel, and how you respond to everything that comes after.

Giving yourself the space to start your morning with intention, with peace, and with something that uplifts your spirit creates a foundation that is much stronger than one built on immediate exposure to chaos. Taking a moment to breathe, to reflect, to express gratitude, or to engage with something that brings you a sense of calm allows you to step into your day from a place of stability rather than reaction. From that space, you are better equipped to handle whatever information you choose to take in later, because you are not receiving it from a place of emotional vulnerability. that is how you *"Stay Happy in the Midst of Havoc"*

This is where the shift begins, in understanding the difference between being informed and being consumed. Staying informed allows you to remain aware of what is happening in the world while still maintaining control over your emotional state. Being consumed, on the other hand, places you in a constant cycle of reacting to things that are outside of your control, creating a sense of overwhelm that does not serve you. Learning to recognize that difference and choosing to protect your peace first is one of the most important steps in navigating a world that often feels chaotic without allowing that chaos to take over your inner state.

It is important to acknowledge that the feeling of being overwhelmed does not mean you are a weak person. It means you are a human being. It means you are aware and that you care about what is happening, not just in your own life, but in the lives of others. That awareness is not something you need to shut off completely. It is something you need to learn how to manage so it does not take over your ability to function, to think clearly, and to experience any sense of calm.

The truth is that control has always been more limited than we like to believe. There have always been things happening beyond our reach, situations unfolding that we had no say in, and outcomes that could not be predicted. What has changed is the level of exposure. You now have access to more information than ever before, and with that access comes the responsibility of deciding how much you allow into your mind and how much you carry with you throughout your day.

Learning how to navigate that responsibility is not about ignoring the world around you. It is about creating boundaries that allow you to stay present in your own life. It is about recognizing when something is within your control and when it is not, and then making a conscious decision not to give your emotional energy to things you cannot influence. That does not make you indifferent. It makes you intentional.

As you begin to understand this, something shifts inside of you. You start to realize that while the world may feel unpredictable, your internal state does not have to mirror that unpredictability. You can create stability within yourself even when things around you are uncertain. You can respond with clarity instead of reacting with fear. You can remain stable and grounded in moments that would have previously pulled you into anxiety.

This is not something that happens overnight. It requires awareness, practice, and a willingness to pause before allowing your emotions to take over. It requires you to recognize when your mind is moving toward fear and gently bring it back to the present moment. It requires you to remind yourself that not every thought needs to be followed, not every fear needs to be entertained, and not every situation requires your emotional involvement.

There will always be things happening in this world that you cannot control. That reality is not going to change. What can change is how much power you give those things over your thoughts, your emotions, and your daily experience. You have more influence over that than you may realize, and learning how to use that influence is what allows you to stay steady, happy and peaceful even when everything around you feels uncertain.

This chapter is not about denying the reality of what is happening in the world. It is about helping you see that even within that reality, there is still space for calm, for clarity, and for peace. That space is not something that appears on its own. It is something you create by becoming aware of what you are allowing into your mind and how you are choosing to respond to it.

As you move forward, begin to notice the moments when the world feels like too much. Pay attention to how your body responds, how your thoughts begin to shift, and how quickly fear tries to take hold. Those moments are not signs that you are failing. They are opportunities to practice something different, to step back, to breathe, and to remind yourself that while you may not control what is happening around you, you still have full and complete control over how you meet it.

Two

The Weight of Living in Constant Fear

There is a quiet kind of exhaustion that comes from living in a state of constant negative awareness, where your mind is always scanning for what could go wrong next, even in moments that should feel safe and calm. It does not always show up in obvious ways, and it does not always announce itself as obvious fear. Instead, it settles into your thoughts, your body, and your daily habits until it begins to feel normal. You wake up, check your phone, and before your feet even touch the ground, your mind is already processing information that has nothing to do with your immediate life, yet somehow manages to affect your emotional state.

Living in a time where the world feels unpredictable has changed the way many people experience their everyday lives. News travels instantly, and with that speed comes a constant stream of information that is often heavy, urgent, and emotionally charged. You are no longer hearing about events days later in a distant, disconnected way. You are seeing them as they unfold, in real time, with images, commentary, and opinions layered on top of one another. That level of exposure creates a sense of closeness to events that may be happening far away, yet feel like they are right at your doorstep.

When you hear that your country is at war, even if you are not directly involved in the decision, there is a shift that happens internally. It may not be loud or immediate, but it is there. It sits in the back of your mind as a reminder that something larger than your daily routine is unfolding. You see images of death and destruction daily on the television. You might find yourself thinking about your own safety in a way you did not before. You start paying more attention to your surroundings, questioning things that once felt ordinary, or feeling a subtle tension that never quite leaves you.

There have been reports in recent years showing how exposure to constant news cycles, especially during times of conflict, can increase anxiety levels significantly, even in individuals who are not directly impacted by the events. Studies have suggested that people who consume hours of news daily during times of crisis are more likely to experience heightened stress levels, difficulty sleeping, and a persistent sense of unease. This is not because they are weak people. It is because the human mind is not designed to process that level of intensity without rest.

The challenge is that stepping away from that information can feel irresponsible. We feel like we should know the dangers of the world. There is a belief that staying informed means staying prepared, and to some extent, that is true. You should know what is happening in the world. You should be aware of your environment and your surroundings. The problem arises when that awareness turns into overexposure, and overexposure turns into a constant state of fear that begins to affect how you live your life.

Fear has a way of convincing you that it is protecting you. It tells you that if you stay alert, if you keep checking, if you keep thinking about every possible outcome, you will somehow be more prepared. In reality, what it often does is take you out of the present moment and place you in a mental space where you are constantly reacting to possibilities instead of responding to what is actually happening in front of you.

There is also a physical component to this that many people overlook. The body does not always know the difference between a real, immediate threat and a perceived one. When you are constantly exposed to stressful information, your body can remain in a heightened state, releasing stress hormones that were meant for short-term survival situations. Over time, this can lead to fatigue, tension, and a feeling that you are always on edge, even when you are sitting in the safety of your own home.

At the same time, life continues to present its own personal challenges, and those moments require your attention in a very real and immediate way. You might be dealing with your child's well-being, your family's needs, your own health, or the responsibilities that come with maintaining a household and a career. These are not distant concerns. These are real, present, and often urgent. When those personal moments intersect with the weight of everything happening in the world, it can feel like there is no separation between what is global and what is personal.

There is a unique kind of pressure that comes from living in both of these realities at the same time. On one side, there are global events that remind you how little control you truly have. On the other side, there are deeply personal moments that require your full presence, your strength, and your ability to respond with clarity. It can feel like there is no space to pause, no space to process, and no space to simply exist without something demanding your attention or your emotional energy.

A moment in my life that lives with me just as clearly happened right in my own home. My grandson, my first grandchild, was just a baby, and what started as something simple turned into something that could have gone very differently. We had given him ice cream, not knowing he would have an allergic reaction. Within moments, he stopped breathing. His skin began to change color, and everything in that room shifted.

There was no time to think about what I did not know. I had never been trained in CPR. I had never been in that situation before. Yet something in me responded. I picked him up, turned him over, patted his back, and did everything I could think of in that moment to help him breathe again. When he finally took that deep breath, it was like the entire room exhaled with him.

Moments like that stay with you. They remind you how quickly life can change, how fragile things can be, and how important it is to be able to stay as calm as possible even when everything feels like it is falling apart. Fear was present in that moment, but it did not take over. It could not, because there was something more important that required my focus.

There are also moments that stretch out over time, moments that do not come and go quickly but instead remain with you day after day. Living for five years with a tumor in my head was one of those experiences. Knowing that something was there, feeling it, hearing it beating like a heart, and still having to show up every day as a mother, a business owner, and a person who chooses to live with intention required a different kind of strength.

There were days when fear could have easily taken over, days when I could have allowed every possible outcome to play in my mind. There were moments leading up to surgery when the risks were explained in ways that could make anyone feel uncertain about what might happen next. Yet even in that space, I made a conscious decision to protect my peace. I chose what I allowed into my mind and what I listened to. I chose how I spent my quiet moments.

Music became part of that process. Sound healing tones became a way to regulate what I was feeling. Creating an environment that supported calm instead of feeding fear was not something I did occasionally. It was something I did intentionally, consistently, and with purpose everyday. That choice made a difference in how I experienced those five years and how I approached the day of surgery itself.

These experiences are not separate from the larger conversation about fear. They are a part of it. They show that fear is not just something that comes from what we see on a screen or hear in the news. It is something that shows up in our homes, in our families, and in our personal lives. It is something that can appear suddenly or stay with us over time.

Many people respond to this by becoming consumed with everything that is happening. They stay plugged into every update, every headline, every piece of information that confirms how uncertain things are. It can feel like staying informed is the responsible thing to do, and to a certain extent, it may be. The problem begins when awareness turns into overload, and an overload of information makes you afraid. At that point, you are no longer simply aware of what is happening. You are carrying it, internalizing it, and allowing it to shape how you feel throughout your day.

That is where the shift has to begin. There is a difference between being informed and being consumed with information, even if they are factual. One allows you to stay connected to reality while still protecting your peace. The other pulls you into a cycle where your emotions are constantly reacting to things you cannot change. Understanding that difference is one of the first steps in learning how to navigate a world that feels out of control without losing yourself in the process. I call this self mastery, and it is a journey but one that will change your life for the better.

It is important to acknowledge that the feeling of being overwhelmed does not mean you are frail and incalculable. It means you are human. It means you are aware. You care about what is happening, not just in your own life, but in the lives of others. That awareness is not something you need to shut off completely. It is something you need to learn how to manage so it does not take over your ability to function, to think clearly, and to experience life to the fullest.

The reality is that much of what happens in this world has never truly been within our control, even though we sometimes live as if it is. There have always been events unfolding beyond our reach, decisions being made without our input, and outcomes that no amount of preparation could fully predict and prepare us for. What feels different now is not necessarily the level of uncertainty, but the constant exposure we have to it. In this age of technology information reaches you instantly, repeatedly, and often without pause, which creates the illusion that you are meant to process all of it and carry it with you throughout your day.

With that level of access comes a responsibility that many people do not realize they have, which is the responsibility to decide what deserves your mental and emotional energy and what does not. This is not about disconnecting from reality or pretending that the world is not experiencing challenges. It is about understanding that you were never meant to absorb everything at once or to internalize every situation as if it were your own.

You were placed on this earth to experience happiness, and although life will present moments of difficulty, that truth does not change. It really can be that simple, even if it does not always feel that way. Havoc can exist in the world around you while peace still exists within you. Chaos can be present in your environment while you still find small, meaningful moments that bring you back to yourself. That might look like stepping outside and feeling the sun on your face, hearing your child laugh in the next room, or allowing yourself to sit in stillness without reaching for your phone. Happiness is not always loud or dramatic. Many times, it is found in quiet moments that you choose to notice.

Creating boundaries with what you take in is an act of self-preservation, not avoidance. It requires you to pause and ask yourself whether something is actually within your ability to influence or whether it is simply something you are witnessing. When you begin to make that distinction, you naturally start to release the pressure of feeling like you have to emotionally respond to everything. That shift does not make you uncaring. It allows you to remain present and effective in your own life without being overwhelmed by things you cannot change.

There are simple practices that can help you return to that place of peace, even on days when life feels heavy. Choosing to begin your morning with something that uplifts your spirit instead of immediately reaching for information that lower your vibration and create stress can change the entire tone of your day. Taking a few moments to breathe deeply and intentionally slows your body down and brings your mind back to the present moment. Listening to music that calms you, whether it is gospel, soft instrumentals, binary beats, or healing frequencies, creates an environment that supports your emotional balance rather than disrupting it.

Spending time outside, placing your feet on the ground, and reconnecting with nature reminds you that not everything is chaotic, that there is still stability in the world, and that you are a part of something much larger than the problems you may be focusing on. I love to journal. I have found that writing your thoughts down can also create clarity, allowing you to release what is weighing on your mind instead of carrying it throughout your day. Even something as simple as shifting your focus toward gratitude, intentionally thinking about what is going right instead of only what feels wrong, begins to change how you experience your reality.

Happiness is not found in controlling everything around you. It is found in how you choose to engage with what is in front of you.

It can be found in the boundaries you set, the thoughts you choose to entertain, and the moments you allow yourself to fully experience without distraction. When you begin to live this way, you realize that peace is not something you have to search for in perfect conditions. It is something you choose to create, moment by moment, even while the world continues to move in ways you cannot control.

As this awareness begins to settle in, you may notice a change in how you experience your daily life. Situations that once pulled you into immediate anxiety no longer have the same grip, and moments that would have once felt overwhelming begin to feel more manageable. Stability starts to come from within you rather than from external circumstances, and that internal steadiness becomes something you can return to even when the world around you feels uncertain.

Developing that kind of awareness takes time and consistency, so be patient with yourself. It is not about forcing yourself to feel calm in every situation, but about building the habit of noticing when your thoughts begin to move in a direction that does not serve you. There is power in pausing before reacting, in choosing not to follow every thought that enters your mind, and in recognizing that not every situation requires your emotional investment.

Life will continue to present events that are outside of your control, and there is nothing you can do about that. What can change is the relationship you have with those situations and circumstances, how much space they take up in your mind, and how deeply they affect your emotional state. You have more influence over that than you may realize, and learning how to use that influence and control is what allows you to remain steady like a rock even when things around you feel unstable.

This is not about denying what is happening or disconnecting from the world. It is about learning how to exist within it without losing your sense of peace. That space for calm does not appear on its own. It is created through your awareness and intention, and through the choices you make about what you allow into your mind and how you respond to it.

As you continue forward, begin to pay attention to the moments when everything feels overwhelming. Notice how quickly your thoughts begin to shift, how your body responds, and how easily fear tries to take the lead. Those moments are not signs that something is wrong with you. They are invitations to pause, to breathe, and to choose a different way of responding. Even when you cannot control what is happening around you, you still have the ability to decide how you handle it, and that is where your power begins.

Three

Life Doesn't Ask for Permission

Life present a truth that many people do not fully accept until they are forced to face it, and that truth is that life does not wait for you to feel ready before it changes everything. It does not pause to consider how you are feeling, what you have planned, or whether you believe you are strong enough to handle what is about to unfold. It moves on its own time, and when it does, it can completely interrupt your sense of normal in a way that demands a response from you immediately. One moment everything feels stable, predictable, and familiar, and the next moment something shifts without warning.

You life blow up and change suddenly and without permission from you. News can arrive that alters everything in an instant. Someone you love can be taken from you. A job you depended on can be gone. A relationship that felt secure can end without explanation. A health diagnosis can appear that forces you to rethink everything you thought you knew about your future. These moments do not send invitations ahead of time. They don't wait for a RSVP. They do not give you the space to prepare yourself emotionally before they arrive. They happen, and when they do, you are left standing in the middle of a reality that feels scary and unfamiliar, trying to process something you never planned for.

In those moments, there is often no luxury of shutting down completely, even if that is what you feel like doing. You cannot disappear, you cannot stay down, and you cannot allow the weight of the situation to completely remove you from your life. There is something within you that has to rise, even if it rises slowly, even if it feels heavy, and even if you are unsure of what to do next. You still have to recalibrate. You have to take a breath, gather your thoughts, and begin to figure out how to move forward in a reality that you did not choose. Life does not stop while you are trying to understand what just happened to you. Responsibilities are still there. The rent is still do, people still need you, and time continues to move whether you feel ready or not. That is what makes these moments so challenging, because while you may need time to process mentally, spiritually, and emotionally, the situation itself may require your attention right away.

There is a belief that many people hold quietly, a belief that if they do everything right, make good decisions, and live carefully, they can avoid these kinds of life-altering moments. That belief feels comforting because it creates a sense of control, a sense that stability can be maintained if you follow the right path. That would be wonderful but the truth is, life does not always operate that way. There are situations that come into your life without warning, without explanation, and without your permission, and when they arrive, they do not ask if you are ready to handle them. Nor do they wait and slow down for you to catch up.

What those moments reveal is not how perfectly you have lived, but how you respond when things do not go according to plan. In the middle of that disruption, there is a choice being made, sometimes without you even realizing it. You can allow the weight of what is happening to take you under completely, to pull you into fear, confusion, and emotional paralysis, or you can begin to reach for something within yourself that allows you to stay present, even while everything around you feels like it is shifting.

That choice is not always easy, and it does not mean that you will not feel the impact of what is happening in your life. It means that somewhere within you, there is a part that can still think, still breathe, and still take one step forward at a time. It is in that space, in that decision to remain present, that you begin to find your footing again, even in the middle of a life that feels like it has been turned upside down.

There was a time in my life when that reality became something I could no longer ignore. My son Justin, my firstborn, my only boy, went missing for three weeks. Saying those words does not fully capture what that experience felt like, because there is no simple way to describe what it means to not know where your child is, to not know if they are safe or what is happening to them, and to wake up every day with that same question still unanswered.

Each day carried a weight that is difficult to explain unless you have lived through something similar. There is a constant loop of negative thoughts that your mind tries to process, questions that have no immediate answers to, and a debilitating level of fear that tries to pull your mind into every possible horrible outcome. Your heart wants to panic, your mind wants to search for certainty, and your body carries the stress of not knowing. Imagine having to get up and care for your other children while one was missing. Having to get dressed brush your teeth and carry on with life while a piece of your soul was broken. It's very hard to do but it is possible.

In that moment, I could have allowed fear to take over completely. I easily could have not been emotionally or mentally present for my three daughters during this time. I could have shut down, withdrawn, and allowed the uncertainty to consume every part of me. That would have been understandable. That would have been human. Yet there was something else present in that within me, something that reminded me that I still had to be a mother to my daughters, that I still had to show up, feed them, love them. I still had to hold a level of stability for the people who depended on me.

That did not mean the fear disappeared. It meant that I had to learn how to carry it without allowing it to break me down. It meant that I had to find moments, even small ones, where I could bring myself back to a place of mental stability. It meant choosing not to let my mind stay in the darkest possibilities, even when those possibilities felt very real. I had to stop reminding myself that while I could not control where my son was in that moment, I could control how I showed up for the rest of my family. As my grandmother Ella Mae would say, I had to "Put it in Gods hands". My son was located three weeks later. He was not in the best shape and had many challenges to face but that indecent taught me that you can be in the absolute worst pain and still get up and function.

Life did not ask me if I was ready for that experience. It did not give me time to prepare or a guide on how to handle it. It simply presented the situation, and I had to respond in real time. That is what life does. It presents situations, and in those situations, your response becomes everything.

These experiences in my life are not isolated from one another. They are connected by a common thread, and that thread is the understanding that life will continue to present moments that you did not plan for, moments that you did not choose, and moments that challenge you in ways you never expected. The question is not whether those moments will come. The question is how you will deal with them when they do.

It is easy to believe that peace is something that exists when everything is going well, when life is calm, and when there are no disruptions. What I have learned is that peace can exist even when those conditions are not present. Peace has to be something you can return to in the middle of hurt, in the middle of fear, and in the middle of situations that do not make sense.

That does not mean you will not feel anything, you will always feel. It does not mean you will not have moments of fear, sadness, or disappointment. It means that those emotions do not have to take over your entire being. You can feel them without becoming them. You can acknowledge what is happening without losing yourself in it.

Life will not always give you time to prepare. It will not always give you answers when you want them. Life may not unfold in a way that feels fair or predictable. What it will do is continue to move, continue to present situations and challenges. It will continue to ask you, in each moment, how you are going to respond to this.

There is a strength that develops when you begin to understand this. There is comfort that comes from knowing that while you cannot control what happens, you can control how you react to it. That stable choice does not remove the challenges in life, but it changes how you experience them. It allows you to move through life with a sense of grounding that is not dependent on everything being perfect.

As you reflect on your own life, think about the moments that came without warning, the situations that changed things for you, and the experiences that required more from you than you thought you had in you to give. Those moments are not just challenges. They are also opportunities to grow and understand yourself, to see how you respond, and to begin to shape that response in a way that supports you instead of working against you.

Life does not ask for permission before it changes everything. It simply moves right along, and in that movement, you are invited to discover a level of strength, self awareness, and intentionality that you may not have known you had. That discovery is not always easy, but it is always valuable. It will change your life for the better, and it is always available to you, no matter what is happening around you.

Four

The Moment Everything Could Break You

There are moments in life that do not just challenge you, they confront you in a way that forces you to decide who you are going to be when everything feels like it is falling apart. These are not ordinary moments. These are the moments where your emotions rise quickly, your thoughts begin to race, and the weight of what is happening feels like it could take you under if you are not careful. These are the moments where fear does not whisper quietly in the background but steps forward and tries to take control of how you think, how you feel, and how you respond.

In those moments, there is often a split second where everything feels suspended, where your mind is trying to process what is happening while your body is already reacting. Your heart may be racing, your thoughts may be scattered, and there is a pull toward panic that feels almost automatic. It is in that space, that very small window of time, where something important happens, even if you are not aware of it at first. That is the moment where you either allow fear to take over completely or you begin, even imperfectly, to gather yourself and respond with intention.

When I think about moments that could have completely broken me, I go back to the experience of my son being missing. There is no way to soften what that feels like. There is no way to make that situation less heavy or less real. Every day that passed without knowing where he was carried a different kind of weight, and there were moments where the fear felt like it could consume everything. There were thoughts that could have easily taken me into a place where I was no longer functioning, where I was no longer present, and where I was no longer able to be what my family needed.

What made that moment so defining was not just the situation itself, but the internal battle that was happening alongside it. There was the part of me that wanted to fall apart, that felt overwhelmed by the uncertainty, and that struggled with the reality of not knowing. At the same time, there was another part of me that understood that I still had to show up, that I still had responsibilities, and that I could not allow myself to disappear emotionally when my daughters still needed their mother.

That internal stress is something many people experience in different ways. It is the space between what you feel and what you choose to do. It is the place where your emotions are real and valid, but your response still matters. It is not about pretending that everything is okay when it is not. It is about recognizing that even when everything feels like it is falling apart, there is still a version of you that can remain steady enough to move forward.

There were moments during those three weeks where I had to consciously bring myself back from thoughts that were not helping me. There were times when my mind wanted to go to the worst possible outcomes, to imagine scenarios that I had no control over, and to sit in that space longer than was healthy. In those moments, I had to remind myself that staying there would not bring my son back, that allowing those thoughts to take over would only take away my ability to function, and that I had to find a way to remain grounded even in the middle of that uncertainty.

That is what makes these moments so powerful. They reveal the patterns of your mind. They show you how quickly you can be pulled into fear, but they also show you that you have the ability to interrupt that pattern. It may not be easy, and it may not happen perfectly every time, but it is possible.

There is another layer to these moments that is just as important, and that is the responsibility you carry for others while you are going through something yourself. When my daughter was injured and I received that call from the school, there was no time to sit in fear for long. My role in that moment required me to be present, to be calm enough to respond, and to be the support system she needed. That did not mean I was not afraid. It meant that my response had to be stronger than my fear.

Being in that position teaches you something very real about your capacity. It shows you that you are capable of holding yourself together even when everything inside you feels shaken. It shows you that there is a part of you that can rise to meet the moment, even when the moment is difficult.

The same truth applies to the experience of my health journey. Living with a tumor for years created many opportunities for fear to take over, especially in moments where the reality of the situation felt closer than usual. Sitting in a doctor's office, hearing about risks, thinking about surgery, and considering what could happen during or after the procedure are all experiences that can push your mind into a place of uncertainty very quickly.

What made those moments defining was not the presence of fear, but the decision to not let that fear dictate how I lived during that time. There were days when I had to consciously choose what I focused on, what I allowed myself to think about, and how I cared for my mental and emotional state. There were moments when I had to bring myself back to the present, to remind myself that not every thought deserved my attention, and to create space for calm even when the situation itself was not calm.

These are the moments that shape you. Not because they are easy, but because they force you to confront how you respond when things are not within your control. They challenge you to develop a level of awareness that allows you to see what is happening internally and make a decision about how you are going to move forward.

There is also something important to understand about breaking points. Many people believe that when they reach a moment that feels overwhelming, it means they are about to break. In reality, those moments often reveal a strength that was already there but had not been fully recognized. They show you that you are capable of more than you thought, that you can navigate situations you never imagined facing, and that you can come through them with a deeper understanding of yourself.

That does not mean the process is comfortable. It does not mean you will not have moments where you feel like you are at your limit. It means that within those moments, there is still a choice, and that choice has the power to shape your experience.

The moment everything could break you is also the moment where everything can begin to change in how you see yourself. It is where you start to understand that your strength is not based on everything going right, but on how you respond when things go wrong. It is where you begin to realize that peace is not something that comes from your circumstances, but something that you create within yourself.

There is a quiet power in that realization. It shifts your focus from trying to control everything around you to learning how to manage what is happening within you. It allows you to approach difficult situations with a different perspective, one that is grounded in awareness and intention rather than fear and reaction.

As you think about your own life, consider the moments that felt like they could have broken you. Think about how you responded, what you learned, and what those moments revealed about your ability to navigate difficulty. Those experiences are not just part of your past. They are part of your foundation. They show you that even when life presents something unexpected, you have the ability to meet it with a level of strength that may not have been visible before.

Moving forward, the goal is not to avoid these moments, because they are a natural part of life. The goal is to approach them with a greater level of awareness, to recognize when fear is trying to take over, and to consciously choose how you are going to respond. That choice may not remove the difficulty, but it will change how you experience it.

There will always be moments that test you, moments that challenge your sense of stability, and moments that require more from you than you expected to give. What matters is not whether those moments come, but how you meet them when they do. That is where your power is, and that is where your peace begins.

Five

You Still Have a Choice

After everything you have experienced in life, after the fear, after the uncertainty and the unexpected situations that life has placed in front of you, there will come a time when you begin to realize something that quietly changes everything. It is not something loud or dramatic, and it does not remove the challenges that exist around you. It is a simple truth, but it carries a weight that can shift the way you move through your life, if you truly accept it. No matter what is happening in the world, no matter what is happening in your personal life, you still have a choice in how you respond.

That realization does not come easily for everyone because it can feel like everything around you is pulling you in a different direction. The world is constantly offering you something to react to. Negative stimuli is everywhere. There is always something negative to focus on, something that can upset you, something that can make you feel uneasy or uncertain. It does not take effort to find it. It is already there, waiting for your attention, waiting for your energy, waiting for you to engage with it.

You can wake up in the morning and immediately step into that space if you choose to. You can reach for your phone, turn on the news, and within minutes begin to absorb information about what went wrong somewhere in the world. You can hear about who was hurt, who lost their life, what conflict has escalated, what tragedy has occurred, and what uncertainty lies ahead. That option is always available, and many people take it without even thinking about what it does to their mind and their emotional state before their day has even begun.

There is another option that exists at that same exact moment, and it requires intention because it is not the one that is automatically presented to you. You can choose to wake up and create a different kind of start to your day. You can choose to take a breath before you take in anything from the outside world. You can choose to sit in a moment of awareness and recognize that you are alive, that you have another day, and that there is something to be grateful for before anything else enters your mind.

That choice may seem small, but it is not. It sets the tone for everything that follows. When you begin your day by allowing negativity to enter first, it has a way of shaping your thoughts, your mood, and your perspective without you even realizing it. When you begin your day with intention, with gratitude, and with a conscious decision to protect your peace, you create a different foundation for how you experience everything that comes after.

Happiness is not something that happens by accident. It is not something that appears only when everything is going well or when life is free of challenges. It is something that requires a decision, and that decision has to be made over and over again. It is made in the small moments, in the way you start your day, in the way you respond to situations, and in the way you choose what you focus on.

There will always be something negative to focus on. That does not require effort. That does not require intention. It exists on its own.

What requires intention is choosing not to stay there, choosing not to allow that to be the only thing that shapes your experience, and choosing to direct your attention toward something that supports your well-being instead of taking away from it.

This does not mean ignoring reality or pretending that difficult things are not happening. It means deciding that while those things exist, they do not have to take over your entire emotional state. It means understanding that you can be aware of what is happening in the world without allowing it to control how you feel throughout your day.

There is a strength in waking up and choosing gratitude even when you know that there are challenges in the world. There is a strength in taking a moment to breathe deeply, to center yourself, and to acknowledge that you are here, that you have another opportunity to live, to love, and to experience life in whatever way you choose. There are millions of people who did not wake up today, and that reality alone is enough to bring a sense of perspective if you allow yourself to sit with it for even a moment.

When you begin to practice this consistently, something starts to shift. You become more aware of the choices you are making throughout your day. You start to notice when your mind is being pulled toward negativity, and you begin to develop the ability to pause before fully engaging with it. That pause is powerful because it creates space for you to choose a different response.

You might find yourself in a situation where something unexpected happens, something that would normally cause you to react immediately. In that moment, instead of allowing your emotions to take over completely, you recognize that you have a choice. You can react in a way that adds to the situation, or you can respond in a way that maintains your sense of calm and clarity. That does not mean the situation changes instantly. It means your experience of it does.

Choosing happiness does not mean forcing yourself to feel something that is not genuine. It means choosing where your focus goes, choosing how you interpret what is happening, and choosing how much space you give to different thoughts and emotions. It is a practice, and like any practice, it becomes stronger the more consistently you engage with it.

There will be days when it feels easier, days when your mind naturally moves toward gratitude and peace. There will also be days when it feels more difficult, when challenges feel heavier, and when negativity seems harder to move away from. Those are the days where the choice matters even more. Those are the days where the practice becomes real, where you have to consciously remind yourself of what you are choosing and why you are choosing it.

You have already experienced moments in your life where you had to make that choice without even realizing it. When your daughter was hurt, when your grandson stopped breathing, when your son was missing, when you were facing your own health challenges, there were moments where you had to decide how you were going to respond. In those moments, you chose to gather yourself, to stay present, and to do what needed to be done. That same ability exists in your everyday life, even when the situation is not as extreme.

What changes is your awareness of it. When you begin to recognize that you have this choice in every moment, you start to use it more intentionally. You begin to understand that happiness is not something that depends on everything being perfect. It is something that can exist alongside difficulty, alongside uncertainty, and alongside the challenges that are a natural part of life.

There is a level of freedom that comes with this understanding. It removes the idea that you have to wait for everything to be right and complete before you allow yourself to feel at peace. It gives you the ability to create moments of calm on purpose for yourself, moments of gratitude, and moments of happiness even when life is not unfolding exactly how you may have wanted it to.

As you move forward, begin to pay attention to the choices you are making throughout your day. Notice what you focus on when you wake up. Notice how you respond to information that comes your way. Notice how quickly your mind moves toward negativity and how often you allow it to stay there without questioning it.

Each of those moments is an opportunity to choose something different. Those moments are a chance to practice returning to a place of serene peace, even when the world around you feels anything but peaceful. That choice may not change everything that is happening around you, but it will change how you experience it, and that is powerful.

Happiness is a choice that you make daily, not once, but over and over again. It is a decision to protect your peace, to guide your focus, and to respond to life in a way that supports your well-being. That choice is always available to you, no matter what is happening, and learning to use it intentionally is what allows you to hold on to your joy and peace even when the world feels like it is falling apart.

Six

Choosing Peace on Purpose

There is a difference between hoping for peace and actually creating it, and that difference becomes clear when you begin to realize that peace is not something that just appears when life calms down, but something that must be built by you, especially when life does not slow down at all. Many people spend their time waiting for the moment when everything settles, when the problems stop coming, when the world feels safe again, and when their personal lives finally give them a break, but what life continues to show us over and over again is that those moments are not guaranteed, and if peace is something you are waiting on, you may find yourself waiting much longer than you expected.

Choosing peace on purpose means understanding that your environment will not always support it, that the world around you may be loud, unpredictable, and sometimes overwhelming, and that your personal life may present challenges that require your attention and your strength, yet even in the middle of all of that, there is still a space within you where calm can exist if you are willing to create it. That space does not happen automatically, and it is not something that stays without effort, but it is something that becomes more accessible the more you practice returning to it.

There were times in my life where I had to make a very clear decision about what I was going to allow into my mind and what I was going to intentionally replace it with, because I understood that if I allowed fear, negativity, and constant noise to take over, it would affect not only how I felt, but how I showed up in every area of my life. Living with a tumor for years, raising children, running my own business for over twenty five years, managing responsibilities, and navigating unexpected situations required a level of emotional and stable presence that I knew I could not maintain if I did not actively choose what I exposed myself to on a daily basis.

When I reflect back now, one of the most defining examples of chaos on a global level was the coronavirus pandemic in 2020. Even years later, the memory of that time still carries weight because of how suddenly everything changed. The world did not slowly shift into uncertainty. It happened almost overnight. One day life felt normal, and the next day people were being told to stay inside their homes, businesses were shutting down, and fear was spreading just as quickly as the virus itself.

At that time, I had never witnessed anything like it. Entire cities felt empty. Restaurants were closed, streets were quiet, and something as simple as going to the grocery store became a stressful experience. People stood in long lines, spaced apart, wearing masks and gloves, unsure of what was safe and what was not. There was constant talk of social distancing, rising case numbers, and the unknown future ahead. It felt like the entire world had paused, yet internally, many people were spiraling because of the uncertainty.

Looking back now from where I stand today, I can clearly see that it was not just a health crisis. It was a mental and emotional test for so many people. Fear and havoc was everywhere, and it was being fed constantly. The news played it on repeat. Conversations centered around it. Social media magnified it. If you were not careful, you could wake up, go to sleep, and spend your entire day surrounded by nothing but anxiety.

Even for someone like myself, who had already committed to a life of positive thinking and personal development, there were moments when that fear tried to find its way in. I remember hearing about how quickly the virus spread from one country to another, how entire places were locked down, and then eventually, it was no longer something happening somewhere else. It became personal. People I knew were getting sick. The distance between me and the situation was gone, and that is when the mental work became real.

That was the moment where everything I believed had to be practiced, not just spoken about. I had to be intentional about what I allowed into my mind. I had to limit my exposure to the news because I could feel how quickly it shifted my emotional state. I had to return to my practices, speaking affirmations of perfect health and peace out loud, over and over again, until my body responded and calmed down. I even had my young daughter repeat them with me, because I understood that peace is something you teach not only with words, but with presence.

There were days when fear tried to rise, and instead of pretending it was not there, I acknowledged it and then made a conscious decision to remove it. That is where I developed what I call "Catch and Cast." I would catch the negative thought the moment it entered my mind, and instead of letting it sit there and grow, I would cast it out and replace it with something that supported my peace. That practice became essential, not optional, because during that time, maintaining a positive state of mind was necessary for emotional survival.

The world was dealing with loss, uncertainty, and major disruption. People were losing jobs, routines were gone, and everyday life felt unfamiliar. It would have been easy to fall into despair, to focus only on what was going wrong, and to allow that to shape my entire experience.

Instead, I made a decision to see that time differently. I chose to view it as an opportunity for growth, for stillness, and for reconnecting with what truly mattered.

Being at home forced a level of reflection that many people had been avoiding. It made me appreciate my space, my family, and the simplicity of life in a way I had not fully experienced before. The inability to go out, shop, or move freely showed me how much we rely on things that are not essential to our peace. I began to detach from those habits and focus on what actually brought me a sense of fulfillment.

That was also a time where my personal practices became even more important. Listening to Tibetan flute music helped calm my mind in ways that words could not. Gospel music reminded me that there was something greater than my circumstances, something steady and unchanging even when the world felt unstable. Sound frequencies like 432 and 528 became tools that allowed me to reset my nervous system and step out of a constant state of alertness.

Looking at that experience now, from the perspective of today, I see it clearly as one of the greatest examples of what this book is about. The world was in chaos. Fear was everywhere. Nothing felt certain. Yet even in the middle of that, I was still able to find moments of peace, moments of gratitude, and moments of clarity.

That is the truth I want you to hold onto. Happiness is not something that waits for the world to calm down. Peace is not something that only exists when everything is going right. Those things are choices, practices, and ways of thinking that you carry with you, even when everything around you feels like it is falling apart.

The pandemic did not just show me how quickly the world can change. It showed me that no matter how much havoc exists outside of me, I still have the ability to choose what happens within me.

Peace is also something that can be found in the simplest, most natural experiences if you allow yourself to engage with them fully. Stepping outside, placing your feet on the ground, and connecting with the earth may seem like something small, but there is something deeply powerful about grounding yourself in that way. Feeling something real beneath you reminds your body that you are here, that you are safe in this moment, and that not everything is as chaotic as your mind might be trying to convince you. That connection gently pulls you out of racing thoughts and brings you back into your body, and within that space, peace becomes much easier to access.

I remember hearing Eckhart Tolle speak about the joy he found in something as simple as sitting on a park bench and observing people as they passed by. There was no urgency, no need to control anything, and no attachment to what was happening around him. There was just presence. That kind of awareness shifts everything, because it shows you that peace is not something complicated or distant. It is something that exists in the moment you choose to be fully present, without allowing your mind to pull you into fear, distraction, or unnecessary worry.

Reading has always been another way for me to redirect my focus, not as an escape from reality, but as a way to nourish my mind with something that supports growth, understanding, and clarity instead of fear. What you allow into your mind matters more than most people realize. When constant negative input is replaced with something that expands your thinking and strengthens your perspective, you begin to notice a shift in how you process your experiences. Situations that once felt overwhelming begin to feel more manageable, and your ability to remain steady becomes something you can rely on instead of something you struggle to find.

Writing, especially writing with purpose, became something even deeper for me. It is not just about putting words on a page. It is about taking everything you have lived through, everything you have learned, and turning it into something that can help someone else. There is peace in that. There is purpose in that. Knowing that your experiences, even the difficult ones, can be used to heal, to guide, and to support someone else creates a sense of meaning that goes beyond the moment you are in.

Breathing is something that is always available to you, yet it is something that many people overlook until they feel overwhelmed. Taking the time to stop, to take a deep breath, and to slow your body down is one of the simplest and most effective ways to return to a place of calm. When your mind is moving quickly and your emotions feel heightened, your breath becomes a tool that can bring everything back to center if you allow it to.

There is also a mindset that has been important in maintaining my peace, and that is the decision to always look for a solution when a problem arises. Problems will continue to come, that is a part of life that does not change, but the way you approach those problems can either add to your stress or help you move through them with clarity. When something happens, instead of allowing my mind to stay in the problem, I shift my focus toward what can be done, what the next step is, and how I can respond in a way that moves things forward.

This does not mean that every problem has an immediate or easy solution, but it does mean that staying stuck in the problem itself does not serve you. It keeps you in a space of frustration, confusion, and emotional heaviness. Looking for a solution, even if it is small, creates movement, and that movement helps you maintain a sense of control and direction even when the situation itself is not ideal.

Choosing peace on purpose is not about creating a perfect life where nothing goes wrong. It is about building a way of living that allows you to return to a place of calm no matter what is happening. It is about having practices, habits, and ways of thinking that support your well-being instead of allowing external circumstances to dictate how you feel every moment of the day.

There will be times when life feels overwhelming, when things do not go as planned, and when challenges come one after another. Those are the moments where your practices matter the most, where the choices you have been making become the foundation you stand on. Peace is not something you search for in those moments. It is something you return to because you have already been building it.

As you reflect on your own life, consider what you are currently allowing into your mind and what you are doing to create moments of calm. Think about the habits you have, the environments you place yourself in, and the ways you respond to stress. There is always an opportunity to shift something, to add something that supports your peace, and to remove something that takes away from it.

This is not about doing everything at once. It is about starting with one intentional choice and building from there. It might be choosing not to check your phone first thing in the morning. It might be taking a few minutes to breathe before starting your day. It might be listening to something that brings you calm instead of something that brings you stress. Each of those choices matters, and over time, they begin to shape how you experience your life.

Peace is not something that exists outside of you waiting to be found. It is something that you create, something that you seek, and return to with conscious intention. Choosing it daily, even when it is not easy, is what allows you to remain steady in a world that will continue to change.

Seven

Training Your Mind to Return to Calm

There is a part of this journey that goes deeper than your environment, deeper than your circumstances, and deeper than anything happening around you, and that is your mind. Everything you experience passes through it first. Every thought, every fear, every reaction, every moment of peace begins there. If your mind is not trained, it will move on its own, and when it does, it often moves toward fear, toward worry, and toward imagining outcomes that have not even happened. When your mind is trained, when you become aware of how it works and how to guide it, everything about your experience of life begins to change.

I wrote a book called *Your Mind is Magic* because I came to understand something that shifted the way I lived my life. The mind is everything. It is not just a part of you that thinks. It is the place where ideas are created, where emotions are formed, and where your perception of reality is shaped. When you understand that, you begin to realize that you are not just experiencing life as it happens. You are experiencing life as your mind interprets it.

That realization brings a level of responsibility, because it means that if your mind is left unchecked, it will create experiences that are not even real, and your body will respond to them as if they are. That is where so much unnecessary suffering comes from. It is not always from what is actually happening. It is from what we are allowing our minds to create.

I remember being a young mother in my twenties, and with that came a level of fear that I had never experienced before. When you have children, there is a part of you that wants to protect them from everything, and that desire can turn into something that takes over your thoughts if you are not careful. I would be at an amusement park with my children, watching them enjoy themselves, and instead of simply being present in that moment, my mind would begin to create scenarios that had not happened and were not happening.

I would imagine something going wrong on a ride, imagine one of my children falling, imagine something happening that would completely change everything. Those thoughts would come in so vividly that my body would respond as if it were real. My heart would race, my chest would tighten, and I would feel a level of fear that had no actual event connected to it. In those moments, I was not responding to reality. I was responding to something my mind had created.

That is what the mind does when it is not guided. It creates, and it does not always create in ways that serve you. It will take a possibility and turn it into something that feels real. It will take a thought and build a story around it. It will take a moment that should be peaceful and fill it with fear if you allow it to move without direction.

What I came to understand over time is that I was creating suffering for myself in moments where there was no real danger. There were enough real challenges in life, enough real situations that required my attention and my strength, and yet I was adding to that by allowing my mind to create additional fear that did not need to exist. I was, in a sense, creating my own emotional distress for situations that had not happened and may never happen.

That awareness was not immediate, and it did not change overnight. It took time for me to recognize the pattern, to see how my thoughts were affecting my emotions, and to understand that I had more control over that process than I initially believed. Once I saw it clearly, I began to practice something that became a foundation for how I maintain my peace, which is the ability to redirect my thoughts, to manipulate ideas in a new direction.

That phrase, manipulating ideas in a new direction, is not about ignoring reality. It is about taking control of how your mind processes what is happening. When a thought comes in that is not serving you, that is creating fear or anxiety without a real reason, you do not have to follow it. You can acknowledge it and then choose to guide your mind somewhere else.

This is where discipline comes in, because the mind will naturally want to go where it has been trained to go. If you have spent years allowing your thoughts to run toward fear, toward worst-case scenarios, or toward negativity, it will take practice to change that pattern. It will not feel automatic at first, but the more you do it, the more natural it becomes.

There is also something important to understand about worry. Most of the things we worry about never actually happen. They exist in our minds, in the stories we create, in the possibilities we imagine, and yet our bodies respond as if those things are real. That means we are experiencing the emotional impact of something that is not even happening, and that can drain your energy, your focus, and your ability to be present in your actual life.

When you begin to train your mind, you start to notice these patterns more clearly. You recognize when a thought is taking you into a space that is not helpful, and instead of allowing it to continue, you bring your focus back to what is real, to what is in front of you, to what you can actually respond to. That shift may seem simple, but it is powerful because it stops the cycle before it takes over.

Training your mind also means choosing what you focus on intentionally. You can focus on everything that is going wrong, everything that could go wrong, and everything that feels uncertain, or you can choose to focus on what is stable, what is present, and what is within your control. That does not mean ignoring challenges. It means not allowing those challenges to be the only thing your mind holds onto.

There is a level of freedom that comes with this understanding. It means that even in the middle of chaos, even in the middle of situations that you did not choose, you still have the ability to create a sense of calm within yourself. That calm does not come from the outside. It comes from how you are choosing to think, how you are choosing to respond, and how you are guiding your mind in each moment.

The mind can work for you or against you. It can create peace or it can create fear. It can support your well-being or it can take away from it. The difference is in how you use it. When you understand that you have the ability to direct your thoughts, to choose what you focus on, and to bring yourself back to a place of calm, you begin to experience life differently.

In the middle of havoc, when everything around you feels uncertain, when the world feels unpredictable, and when personal challenges arise, your mind becomes the place where your experience is shaped. That is where you decide whether you are going to be consumed by what is happening or whether you are going to remain steady within it.

You can choose to be calm. You can choose to focus on happiness. You can choose to guide your thoughts in a way that supports your peace. Those choices may not change what is happening around you, but they will change how you experience it, and that is where your power is.

As you move forward, begin to pay attention to your thoughts without judgment. Notice where your mind goes when you are not directing it.

Notice the patterns, the habits, and the tendencies that show up. Once you are aware of them, you can begin to change them. You can begin to guide your mind in a way that aligns with the kind of life you want to experience.

Your mind is not something that should be left to run on its own. It is something that can be trained, something that can be guided, and something that can become one of your greatest tools when you learn how to use it intentionally. That is where peace begins, not outside of you, but within you, in the way you think, in the way you respond, and in the way you choose to experience your life.

Eight

Holding Yourself Together for the People Who Need You

Often you will find that there is a different kind of strength that is required when you are not just responsible for yourself, but for other people who are looking to you for stability, for safety, and for reassurance in moments where everything feels uncertain. It is one thing to go through something difficult on your own and take the time you need to process it, but it is something entirely different when you are in a situation where others depend on you to stay grounded even when you feel shaken inside.

That kind of responsibility does not announce itself in advance. It shows up in real time, often in moments where you would much rather pause, take a breath, and allow yourself to feel everything that is happening. Instead, you find yourself stepping into a role that requires clarity, quick thinking, and emotional control because the people around you need you to be steady.

There is no training for that. There is no perfect preparation. There is only the moment, and in that moment, you either rise into that responsibility or you allow fear to take over in a way that affects everyone around you.

I sincerely believe that 90% of the people who refer to themselves prayer warriors are missing the key elements of effective prayer. Have you ever noticed how many people you know pray endlessly for hours upon hours, yet their lives still seem to be void of the things they pray for?

I am certain that is because ineffective prayer is pointless. It's like planting a seed in a dry desert field and never watering it. Ineffective prayers are prayers to God that are followed with fear and doubt. When we ask God for something, but deep down we are convinced we don't actually believe we can have what we are asking for, the prayer is useless.

We must "believe in things unseen," despite the logical brain attempting to rationalize our desire. We must believe it's possible, and better yet, believe it is already done. The statement, "All things are possible," means just that: all things, not just the ones we've figured out how to attain. For example, you have been praying to God for a new three-bedroom home, but the minute you attempt to focus that thought and create the visual needed to manifest this new home, your logical brain says, "You don't make enough money," or "Your credit is bad," etc. These are the negative, counteractive thoughts we must not allow to persist. Cast them out and continue to visualize your desires.

Miracles are not logical. It is simply for us to plant the seed, believe that what we desire is indeed possible and move forward and let the harvest grow. It seems we counteract the things we desire by changing our minds, changing our thoughts, and talking ourselves out of all the things we are praying to God for. It's normal behavior. We have all done it, but the key is learning to recognize when your mind has begun operating in reverse so you can instantly refocus it.

The very second that self sabotage begins, stop it!

I also believe that the effective prayers of our ancestors can protect us and generations to come. I am certain that my beloved Texan grandmother's prayers over my sister and me have shielded us from harm on many occasions. For example, I was chased out of a crab restaurant at gunpoint in 2009. I was paralyzed with fear. I remember running out the door when my knees buckled and I slammed both knees onto the hard concrete. Somehow, I got up and continued to run, still so petrified that I fell once more. The masked gunman seemed to be distracted by my running out. Although he had the gun pointed at the cashier as she attempted to comply with his demands for money, he stopped and moved his focus from her to me as I ran out the door. He turned and ran out behind me. The second time I fell onto my back on the side of the building as he walked up and pointed the gun directly in my face.

Everything seemed to be moving in slow motion. Defenseless and on my back, I stared down the barrel of the gun. Knowing that I was helpless at this point. I stared directly through the holes in the ski mask he wore and into his eyes, too afraid to even scream. It couldn't have been more than a few seconds of deafening silence, but it felt like so much longer. He didn't try to rob me for the car keys, cell phone or camera I was holding. Instead, he stared right back at me, and just from the expression in his eyes, I could see him contemplate whether or not he should shoot me. I could literally see him trying to decide. He shifted his gaze to the right, and then locked back onto me. Then, miraculously, he lowered the gun and ran off.

Of course, I can only speculate about what happened, but I choose to interpret that situation as God saying, "No, not her and not today. I still have so much work for her to do." I sincerely believe that it was God and the persistent effective prayers of protection from my late grandmother that made him walk away. Since then, I have always felt that my life was spared that day by the Divine Source because there is so much that I have to do before I leave this earth. Writing this book is one of my destined purposes. I have been walking and talking in my calling ever since.

That moment could have broken me. Being face to face with death, feeling completely helpless, and knowing that everything could end in a matter of seconds is something that could stay in your mind and replay over and over again if you allow it. It could have turned into fear that followed me everywhere, into anxiety that controlled how I moved through my life, and into a constant sense of danger even in safe spaces.

Instead, I had to make a decision about how I was going to carry that experience. I had to choose whether I was going to relive it or whether I was going to learn from it and move forward. That choice did not remove what happened, but it changed how much power it had over me.

Jamaica February 2020

In February 2020, while on a vacation in Montego Bay, Jamaica with my friends and family, we experienced something that no tourist should ever have to endure. We were so excited to arrive because we rented this huge five-bedroom villa. We had our children with us and could not wait to experience Jamaica's finest. When we arrived at this beautiful villa we were so pleased. The house was grand, and the AirBnB pictures did not do it justice. We had our own private cook and driver for the entire seven-day vacation. We could not have been happier. They even arranged for a crib for my eight-month-old grandson.

This all went downhill quickly, starting with our return to the villa on day two after a day of shopping to find a strange man there who claimed to be the new homeowner. He said he was there to see who was occupying his property. We assured him that we arranged to rent this property in December of 2019 and had paid in full for ten guests for seven days. He told me personally that his lawyer told him to throw us out, but he had decided to allow us to stay. This was very unsettling.

In the middle of this unexpected drama we were also faced with the fact that we had given the cook $360 USD to go shopping for groceries for the week and she had only purchased approximately $80 worth of groceries and refused to provide a receipt.

A series of other unacceptable things happen that resulted in us deciding on day five to move into another house that was provided for us by the previous owner at her expense, being that she felt responsible for the situation because she never informed us that the home had been sold.

When we returned home on the fifth day and packed our bags, we told the house sitter, Sean, that we were leaving and would not be staying the last two days. We were told that we could not leave. The new homeowner, His Excellency Crown Bishop Dr. Kevin O. Smith, gave the order to chain the gate and lock us inside the property. I politely asked Sean to unchain the gate and let the van in to retrieve us and our suitcases and he said, "No." He told me that I was rude for not giving him notice that we were leaving early, and that he would not open the gate because we were scheduled to leave on February 26th, and it was only the 24th. I was in shock, but once it was clear that he was not going to open the gate and we were now apparently prisoners, I began to scream and gather my friends and family. We ran down the driveway to the front gate and I noticed there was a 3ft fence that we could climb over and exit the property. Although it would not be easy because there were nine of us; five adult women, one of which was my twenty-five-year-old daughter who was two months pregnant at the time. There were also eleven-year-old twins, my seven-year-old daughter and my eight-month-old grandson.

Out of sheer disbelief, panic, and rage we climbed the fence along with several heavy suitcases with the help of Junior, our driver. We then went directly to the Coral Gardens Police Department.

I tell you this horrible story for one reason and one reason only: even during horrific times, we must attempt to maintain a positive mental attitude. We were clearly in a situation that was beyond our control, and to this day, I have no idea what their intent was by chaining us in, but I'm so grateful I acted quickly and that we all made it back to America safely.

In that moment, I did not have the option to fall apart. There were children there. There were people looking to me for direction. There were decisions that needed to be made quickly, and those decisions required clarity, not panic. That is what it means to hold yourself together for the people who need you. It means that even when fear is present, you do not allow it to take over in a way that puts others at risk.

That does not mean you are not afraid. It means you choose not to let fear lead.

There is a strength in that kind of control, and it is not something that comes from pretending everything is okay. It comes from understanding that in certain moments, your role is bigger than your feelings. Your responsibility is bigger than your fear. Your presence is required in a way that demands focus, awareness, and action.

After those moments pass, after the danger is gone, after everyone is safe, that is when you allow yourself to process what happened. That is when you acknowledge the fear, the anger, and the emotional weight of what you experienced. Even then, there is still a choice to be made. You can stay in that moment mentally, replay it, relive it, and allow it to continue affecting you, or you can begin the process of healing and moving forward.

Holding yourself together for others does not mean you ignore yourself. It means you understand when it is time to lead and when it is time to heal. Both are necessary. Both are part of maintaining your peace.

Life will continue to present moments where people need you to be steady, where your response matters, and where your ability to remain calm can make all the difference. Those moments will not always be easy, but they will always reveal something about your strength, your awareness, and your ability to rise when it matters most.

Nine

Finding Gratitude in the Middle of Pain

Pain has a way of narrowing your focus, pulling your attention directly to what is wrong, what is missing, or what feels unfair, and in those moments it can feel almost impossible to see anything beyond the discomfort you are experiencing. Pain demands to be felt, and there is nothing wrong with acknowledging that, but if you stay there too long without creating space for anything else, it can begin to shape your entire perspective in a way that makes it difficult to recognize that even in the middle of hardship, there is still something to hold onto.

Gratitude in those moments does not come naturally, and it does not appear without intention. It is not something that shows up on its own when everything feels heavy. It is something that must be searched for, something that must be chosen, and something that must be practiced even when it feels like the last thing you want to do. That is what makes it powerful, because choosing gratitude in the middle of pain shifts your focus in a way that allows you to see more than just what is wrong.

There have been many moments in my life where I had every reason to focus only on what hurt, what scared me, or what felt out of my control, and yet something in me understood that if I stayed in that space, it would only make the situation feel heavier than it already was. When my daughter was injured and I received that call from the school, the initial reaction was fear, and rightfully so. Hearing that your child is being transported by ambulance is not something you prepare for, and it is not something that feels small in any way.

In that moment, my mind could have gone to the worst possible outcomes, and for a brief second, it tried to. That is what the mind does. It searches for meaning, it tries to anticipate what could happen next, and it often moves toward fear when there is uncertainty. Yet even in that moment, there was another layer of awareness that began to form, one that reminded me to stay present, to focus on what was actually happening, and to recognize that while the situation was serious, it could have been worse.

That is where gratitude begins, not in denying what is happening, but in recognizing that even within the situation, there is something to be thankful for. My daughter's injury, as painful as it was, was not something more severe. It was not something that changed her life permanently. It was something that could be treated, something that could heal, and something that we could move through together.

That shift in perspective does not remove the pain, but it changes how you carry it. It allows you to hold both realities at the same time, the reality that something difficult has happened and the reality that there is still something to be grateful for within it. That balance is what keeps you from being completely consumed by the situation.

The same understanding applies to so many of the experiences we go through, even the ones that feel overwhelming at first. When I think about the families who have lost their homes, who have been displaced, and who are fighting to rebuild their lives after events that were completely outside of their control, it is easy to focus on what was lost. It is easy to see the devastation, the frustration, and the emotional weight of starting over.

At the same time, there are layers within those situations that hold something else, something that can be easy to overlook if you are only focused on what is gone. There is the fact that lives were spared. There is the opportunity to rebuild, even though it may not be easy. There is the presence of community, of support, and of resilience that begins to show itself in ways that would not have been seen otherwise.

Gratitude does not mean you ignore the loss. It means you allow yourself to see beyond it, to recognize that even in the middle of something difficult, there are still elements of life that remain, still pieces that can be appreciated, and still reasons to continue moving forward.

There was a time in my life when I was dealing with my own health situation, living with something that could have easily taken my mind into a place of constant fear. That experience could have been defined entirely by uncertainty, by worry, and by the unknown. Instead, I had to find a way to live within it without allowing it to take over everything.

Gratitude in that situation did not come from the condition itself. It came from the ability to still wake up each day, to still be present for my family, to still have the strength to continue living my life, and to still have the opportunity to experience moments of peace even while knowing that something was there. That perspective allowed me to move through that time with a level of calm that would not have been possible if I had focused only on what could go wrong.

There is something important to understand about gratitude. It is not about minimizing your experience or pretending that things are easier than they are. It is about expanding your awareness so that you are not only focused on one part of the situation. It is about allowing yourself to see the full picture, which includes both the challenges and the things that still hold value, still hold meaning, and still bring a sense of light into your life.

When you begin to practice gratitude intentionally, it becomes easier to access even in moments where it feels difficult. It becomes something you return to, something that grounds you, and something that reminds you that no matter what is happening, there is still something within your life that is worth appreciating.

There is also a level of healing that comes with gratitude. When you focus only on pain, it has a way of keeping you in that space, of replaying the experience, and of holding onto the emotional weight longer than necessary. When you begin to introduce gratitude into that space, it creates a shift, one that allows you to process what happened without staying stuck in it.

That does not mean the process is immediate. It does not mean you will instantly feel better or that everything will make sense right away. It means that you are giving yourself another perspective, another way to see the situation, and another path to move forward that is not rooted only in pain.

As you reflect on your own life, think about the moments that were difficult, the situations that challenged you, and the experiences that felt overwhelming at the time. Within those moments, there are often pieces that you may not have noticed right away, things that you can now look back on and recognize as something that helped you, something that strengthened you, or something that allowed you to grow in a way you did not expect.

Gratitude is not about waiting for everything to be perfect before you allow yourself to feel it. It is about choosing to see what is still present, what is still working, and what is still meaningful even when life is not unfolding exactly as you planned.

That choice has the power to shift your entire experience. It does not remove the challenges, but it changes how you move through them. It allows you to carry your experiences in a way that does not weigh you down completely, and it gives you the ability to find moments of peace even in situations that are not easy.

Ten

Becoming Unshakable in a Shaking World

There comes a point in your journey where everything you have experienced, everything you have learned, and every moment that has tested you begins to come together in a way that changes how you see yourself and how you move through the world. It is not that life suddenly becomes easy or that challenges stop appearing, because they do not. It is that you begin to understand yourself in a deeper way, a spiritual way, and with that understanding comes a level of emotional stability that is not easily shaken.

Being unshakable does not mean that you never feel hurt, pain or fear. It doe not meant that you never experience instability, or that you are unaffected by what happens around you. It means that those things no longer have the power to completely take you over. It means that even when life presents something difficult, which it will, there is a part of you that remains calm, a part of you that knows how to return to calm, and a part of you that understands that you will get through whatever life brings your way.

Everything you have gone through has been preparing you for that.

It has been teaching you and strengthening you from the inside. Every moment that required you to hold yourself together, every situation that forced you to choose how you were going to respond, and every experience that pushed you beyond what you thought you could handle has contributed to the strength you now have within you today.

There was a time when certain situations might have completely overwhelmed you, when fear might have taken over more quickly, and when it may have felt like you had less control over your own thoughts and your emotions. As you have grown and learned, and practiced returning to your place of peace, something has shifted in you as it did in me. You have begun to see that you are not as fragile as you once thought. You are not impulsive and reactive. You are capable of more than you realized, and you have a level of resilience that continues to develop with each experience you go through Holding on to your joy and peace when the world is falling apart is not by any means easy. But learning how to do it will make a significant different in your quality of life.

The world will continue to change. Wars and pandemics may still come. Fires will still burn and leaders we trust will still be corrupt. That is not something that can be avoided. What can be developed is your ability to move through those moments without losing yourself in the process. Create peaceful positive practices for yourself. Choose things that make you laugh.

You may have faced situations that could have broken you, and you are still here reading this book. You have experienced moments that could have taken your peace completely, and yet you have found ways to return to it. You have learned how to pause, how to breathe, how to shift your focus, and how to guide your mind in a way that supports your well-being.

That is what makes you unshakable. It is not the absence of difficulty or certainty of a perfect world. It is the presence of awareness, the presence of intention, and the presence of a mindset that allows you to navigate whatever comes your way.

There is also something important about the way you choose to live moving forward. You no longer have to wait for everything to be ideal before you allow yourself to feel at peace. You do not have to depend on external circumstances to bring you internal happiness. You have the ability to create moments of calm, moments of gratitude, and moments of happiness even when life is not unfolding exactly as you envisioned it.

That is where your power is. It is the true test of your ability to choose. It is your ability to respond, favorably and return to love and peace no matter what is happening around you.

As you continue your journey, there will always be new experiences, new challenges, and new moments that require your attention and your strength. Now you will not approach them the same way you did before, because you now have tools, awareness, and a deeper understanding of how to maintain your peace.

You are not at the mercy of everything that happens around you. It is not you job to carry the load of every piece of negativity that exists in the world. You are not obligated to allow fear to take over your thoughts and your emotions. You can stop it in it's tracks. You now know that you have a choice in how you experience your life, and that choice is something you can use every single day. I always say to the young women I mentor "You are Great, and this is Your Life to Create". So Lets Go!

When you understand that and remember and accept your greatness, you begin to move differently in the world. You begin to approach situations with a calm mind and clarity, with more intention and confidence in your ability to handle whatever comes your way. You begin to see yourself as someone who is capable and in full control, someone who is strong, and someone who can remain happy and peaceful even when things in the world are out of control.

This is not the end of your journey. It is the beginning of a new beautiful way of living, one where you are no longer controlled by what happens around you, but are instead guided by how you choose to respond to it.

No matter what is happening in the world, no matter what challenges come your way, and no matter how uncertain things may feel at times, there is always a place within you that can remain happy, calm, grounded, and at peace.

Eleven

Conclusion

Holding On to Yourself in a World That Won't Always Be Gentle

If you have made it to this point, it means something inside of you is still searching for peace and happiness, still reaching for something steady, and believing that even in a world filled with chaos and havoc, there is a way to remain happy, grounded, whole, and emotionally intact. That matters more than you may realize, because it means that no matter what you have faced, no matter what you are currently carrying, and no matter what may come, there is still a part of you that refuses to give up on yourself. You now understand that happiness is a choice that we all can make daily.

Life has a way of presenting moments that do not make sense to us, moments that feel unfair, and moments that can shake you in ways you never expected. You have already experienced some of those moments. You have already faced situations that tested your strength, your patience, your faith, and your ability to keep going. There were times when you did not know how things would turn out, times when fear tried to take over, and times when it would have been easier to shut down than to keep showing up.

Yet here you are. Still here determined to sustain happiness and peace.

That is not something small, or something to overlook. That is proof that there is a strength and a strong will within you that exists even when you do not feel it, even when you question it, and even when life feels heavier than usual. That strength is not about never feeling fear or never being affected by what happens around you. It is about your ability to continue, to adjust, and to find your way back to yourself no matter what you are facing.

There will always be things in this world that shake us up. There will always be situations and circumstances that unfold without your permission, challenges that arise without warning, and moments that ask more of us than we feel ready to give. That is a part of life that does not change. What changes is how we all navigate those moments, how we carry them, and how much of ourselves we allow them to take from us.

You have learned that happiness is not something that waits for perfect conditions. It is something that is chosen, protected, and practiced. It is found in the way you start each and every day, in the way you guide and control your thoughts, and in the way you respond when life does not go as planned. It is something you can always return to, even when it feels difficult at first, even when it requires effort, and even when everything around you is pulling you in several different directions.

You have also seen that your mind is powerful, that it can create fear just as easily as it can create peace, and that learning how to guide it is one of the most important things you can do for yourself. The thoughts you allow to stay, the focus you choose to hold, and the way you interpret your experiences all shape how you feel. When you take control of that process, you begin to experience life differently, not because everything has changed around you, but because you have changed.

There is something deeply important about the way you continue to show up for others as well. The moments where you had to hold yourself together, where you had to be strong for your children, your family, and the people who depend on you, those moments reveal a level of strength that cannot be taught, only lived. You did not always have time to process your emotions in those situations. You did not always have the luxury of falling apart. You stepped into the moment and became what was needed, and that is something that deserves to be recognized and applauded.

At the same time, you are allowed to care for yourself too. You must take the time to breathe, to reset, and to return to a place of calm after everything you have carried. Strength does not mean ignoring your own personal needs. It means knowing when to lead and knowing when to heal, understanding that both are necessary, and allowing yourself the space to do both.

As you close this book, I want you to understand something clearly and deeply. You are not powerless. You are not at the mercy of everything that happens around you. You do not have to carry every piece of fear, every piece of negativity, or every piece of uncertainty that exists in this world.

Happiness is a choice. You have a choice in how you think. Whether you focus on negative or positive thoughts. You have a choice in how you respond. Whether you stop, think and breath first or impulsively react first. You have a choice in how you protect your peace. You choose who's energy you allow around you.

That choice is available to you every single day, in every moment, no matter what is happening around you. It may not always feel easy to make that choice, and there will be times when you have to remind yourself of it, but it is always there.

There will be days when life feels lighter, when peace comes more easily, and when everything seems to flow in a way that feels natural. There will also be days when things feel heavier, when challenges arise, and when you have to work a little harder to return to that place within yourself. Both of those days are part of the journey, and neither one defines you as a whole.

What truly defines you is not how easy your life has been or how perfectly everything has unfolded for you, but your willingness to keep going each day, to keep returning to yourself, and to hold onto your sense of peace even when life feels chaotic. There is a quiet strength in continuing forward when things are unclear, in staying grounded when your emotions are being pulled in many different directions, and in deciding that no matter what is happening around you, you will not abandon yourself in the process.

There is no requirement to be perfect in this journey, and there is no expectation that you will always have the answers or handle every situation without feeling the weight of it. Life is going to challenge you, and there will be moments that test your patience, your strength, and your emotional stability. Don't give up. you will get though those times. What matters is not that you avoid those moments, but that you move through them with grace and intention. It is important that you allow yourself to feel things deeply without becoming consumed by them, and that you continue to choose a response that supports your peace rather than taking it away.

Each day presents a new opportunity to guide your mind in a positive direction, to decide where your focus will rest, and to choose how you will experience what is in front of you. There will always be reasons to fall into fear, reasons to focus on what is going wrong, and reasons to feel overwhelmed by the state of the world. At the same time, there is always the option to shift your awareness and recognize the amazing beauty of this world. Always try to find something to be grateful for, and return to a place within yourself that remains steady regardless of external circumstances.

Within all of us exists a space that is not easily shaken, a place where our awareness, our peace, and our ability to choose how we respond all come together as one. That space does not depend on everything being the way we desire it, and that space does not disappear when life becomes difficult. It becomes stronger each time you return to it, each time you remember your greatness, each time you pause and take a breath instead of reacting, and each time you remind yourself that you still have control over how you show up in this world.

Let this become something you carry with purposeful, deliberate intention, not as a temporary feeling or a passing thought, but as a new way of living that you return to again and again. The practice of choosing happiness and peace, guiding your thoughts, and grounding yourself in gratitude and love is not something you do once. It is something that becomes permanent part of who you are. It becomes something that supports you through both the calm moments and the challenging ones.

No matter what is happening in the world, no matter what challenges arise, and no matter how uncertain things may feel at times, there is always a path back to your true God-given nature. That return is always available to you. That road is always open and it is in that return that you will find your peace waiting for you.

About the Author

SaBrina Fisher Reece was once known throughout California as "The Braid Queen." For more than twenty-six years, she owned and operated the legendary Braids By SaBrina, a celebrated salon and school on Adams Boulevard in Los Angeles. It grew into the largest and most influential braiding establishment in the city, where artistry, empowerment, discipline, and community came together in powerful ways. Her success was entirely self-made, built through perseverance, resilience, and vision, often without consistent external support or validation.

As she stepped into the second half of her life, SaBrina felt a deeper calling unfolding within her. The story behind her success was not just one of entrepreneurship, but one of faith, healing, self-trust, and spiritual awakening. Early experiences of abandonment and profound personal loss led her inward, where she began the real work of emotional healing and inner mastery. What started as creative expression evolved into purposeful transformation.

Today, SaBrina writes self-help books rooted in emotional healing, personal growth, and spiritual awareness. Blending lived experience with motivational insight and metaphysical understanding, she explores themes of balance, resilience, self-mastery, and the unseen forces that shape human thought and behavior. Through her writing and motivational speaking, she guides readers toward deeper self-awareness, renewed confidence, and lives that feel intentional and aligned from the inside out.

She is the author of numerous self-help and transformational works, including *My Spiritual Smile, Kicking Depression In the Butt, Your Mind Is Magic, Perfectly Positive, Living Life on a Higher Frequency, Spiritual Balance, Angry World, Become Your Own Cheerleader,* God is Not a Man: Rediscovering the Divine Balance of Masculine and Feminine Within Us All, *Self Sabotage, How to Get Exactly What You Want From God, When I Say "I Am"*, and the popular Ebooks: *Imagine: Learn How to Use Your Imagination to Design the Life You Desire, You're Not Religious -You're Spiritual-I Get It: Bridging the Gap Between the Two, , Take A Breath With Bri: The Power of Intentional Breathing, Is This Why They Burned The Books?: Buried Wisdom From The Past.*

Her passion for sound and frequency has led her to explore the healing power of crystal sound bowls, tuning forks, and flow chimes, tools designed to help harmonize the body, mind, and spirit. Now residing in the enchanting landscapes of New Mexico, "The Land of Enchantment," she offers Sound Vibration Sessions that invite others to slow down, breathe deeply, and reconnect with their higher selves. While she embraces these modalities, she reminds her students and readers that there is no single path to peace. Every journey is sacred, and every sincere method of connecting with the Divine carries value.

Above all, SaBrina is a devoted mother of four, Justin, Joi, Jayden, and Journey, and a proud grandmother to Raiden Jesse and Rio Jordan.

Watching them, and those she teaches, awaken to their divine potential remains her greatest joy.

Her message is simple and enduring: we are each born with divine energy, a God-given power to create, to heal, and to live fully. The goal is not perfection, but peace. The journey is not to escape life, but to embrace it, to use positive tools to take control of the mind and become the master of your fate.

You can connect with me on:

https://www.facebook.com/BooksBySaBrinaFisherReece

Also by SaBrina Fisher Reece

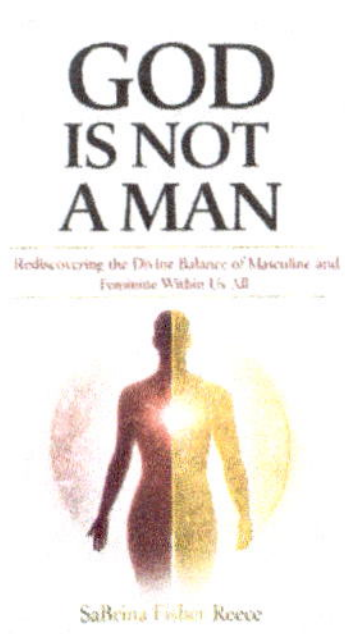

God is Not a Man

Is God exclusively male, or have we limited the image of the divine through tradition and culture?

In *God Is Not a Man: Rediscovering the Divine Balance of Masculine and Feminine Within Us All*, SaBrina Fisher Reece explores a powerful and often overlooked truth: divine source is not confined to gender. Drawing from scripture, ancient wisdom, global spiritual traditions, personal travel experiences, and modern psychological insight, this book challenges inherited assumptions while honoring faith.

Reece takes readers on a journey through Egypt, Greece, Indonesia, and Peru in search of a deeper understanding of God. Along the way, she examines universal law, the balance of masculine and feminine energy, and the spiritual maturity required to hold faith without limiting it. With clarity and conviction, she reveals how imbalance in our understanding of divine image has shaped theology, identity, and culture.

This book offers healing for women who have felt spiritually secondary and freedom for men who have felt pressured to suppress emotional depth. It speaks to the seeker who longs for truth without abandoning reverence. It affirms that strength and tenderness, authority and compassion, structure and intuition are not opposites but complementary expressions of one infinite source.

Rather than rejecting tradition, *God Is Not a Man* expands it. Rather than attacking faith, it deepens it. Readers will come away empowered, grounded, and more comfortable in their own wholeness, understanding that divine image is far greater than any single label.

For those ready to move beyond limitation and into balance, this book offers clarity, humility, and spiritual confidence.

How to Balance Good and Evil
Understanding the Polarity of Human Nature and Choosing the Higher Path

What if "good" and "evil" are not distant forces fighting somewhere outside of you-but daily choices happening quietly within you?

In this powerful and deeply personal book, SaBrina Fisher Reece explores the truth about human nature: we are all born into a world of polarity. Light and shadow. Compassion and cruelty. Fear and love. The tension is not proof that you are broken—it is proof that you have been given free will.

This book does not label people as evil. It does not shame anger, frustration, or human imperfection. Instead, it teaches you how to recognize the internal tug-of-war we all experience and how to consciously choose the higher path without denying your humanity.

Through raw personal stories, leadership lessons, parenting moments, business experiences, and spiritual insight, SaBrina reveals how polarity shows up in everyday life-at work, in relationships, in traffic, in conflict, and even in your own thoughts. She demonstrates that self-regulation, compassion, emotional control, and imagination are powerful tools that help you move toward integrity instead of impulse.

You will learn:

How to understand the "dark side" without being ashamed of it

Why emotional control is a life-saving skill

How small daily choices shape your character

The difference between reacting and choosing

How compassion creates a better world without tolerating abuse

Why discipline is required to consistently choose your higher self

This book is for men, women, and young people who want to grow spiritually without judgment or religious condemnation. It is for those who understand that while horrific acts exist in the world, no one is born destined for darkness. We are given a choice every day.

You wake up at the center of the pole.

The direction you lean becomes the person you become.

If you are ready to understand yourself more deeply, lead with your heart, and consciously choose the higher side of who you are, this book will guide you there.

Balance & Focus 2 Book Series

SaBrina Fisher Reece is the creator of the Balance and Focus Framework, a transformational approach to building emotional stability and disciplined clarity in everyday life. Through her books, speaking, and coaching, she teaches that balance is the foundation and focus is the force that shapes results. Her work helps individuals strengthen their inner world so they can build a more intentional and aligned life.

Blending spiritual awareness with practical structure, her work helps readers stabilize their internal world and direct their energy with intention.

She helps individuals cultivate emotional steadiness, mental discipline, and intentional living in every area of life.

Get Both Books Here:

https://mybook.to/TheBalanceFocusSeries

Pressure Down Plates Up CookBook
Delicious Meals for Lower Blood Pressure

High blood pressure does not mean giving up flavor.

It does not mean bland food, boring meals, or feeling restricted at the dinner table. It means learning how to cook smarter, season differently, and nourish your body in a way that supports your heart.

In *Pressure Down Plates*, you will discover delicious, satisfying meals designed to help lower blood pressure naturally-without sacrificing taste. This cookbook focuses on simple ingredients, practical swaps, and flavorful combinations that make heart-healthy eating feel enjoyable instead of overwhelming.

Inside you'll find:

Low-sodium meals packed with flavor

Smart seasoning alternatives that don't rely on excess salt

Simple recipes for busy weeknights

Wholesome ingredients that support heart health

Easy dishes the whole family will love

Whether you are newly diagnosed, managing long-term hypertension, or simply wanting to be proactive about your health, this book gives you meals you can actually look forward to eating.

Taking care of your heart should feel empowering-not limiting.

Lower the pressure. Lift your plates. Enjoy your food again.

Take a Breath with Bri (Ebook)

What if the one thing you've been doing your entire life... is the one thing you've never truly learned to do?

You breathe every single day. Over 20,000 times. Yet most of those breaths happen unconsciously, shallow and rushed, mirroring a world that rarely slows down.

In *Take a Breath With Bri,* motivational speaker Bri Reece invites you to rediscover the most powerful, accessible tool you already possess: your breath.

For decades, Bri lived a fast-paced life, running a business for over thirty years without ever pausing to understand the importance of intentional breathing. It wasn't until her fifties that she slowed down long enough to realize that breath is more than survival. It is regulation. It is clarity. It is peace. It is power.

Blending science, spirituality, and personal experience, this uplifting and deeply personal guide explores:

The medical benefits of slow, controlled breathing

How breath regulates anger, anxiety, and emotional overwhelm

Why impulsive reactions can destroy lives - and how one conscious breath can prevent it

Ancient breathing wisdom from Egypt, India, Tibet, the Andes, and beyond

Simple, practical breathing exercises you can begin immediately

How to teach children emotional regulation through breath

The spiritual significance of breath as the life force within us all

Each chapter gently reminds you that before reacting, before speaking, before escalating, you can pause and take one intentional breath.

Bri's signature message, "Take a breath with Bri, and you will see that everything will be all right," has helped thousands regulate their emotions and find calm in moments of chaos. Now, through this book, she teaches you how to create that steadiness for yourself - anytime, anywhere.

This is not a medical manual. It is a life manual.

It is for the parent who wants to model calm.

It is for the young person overwhelmed by anxiety.

It is for the individual who reacts too quickly.

It is for the spiritual seeker.

It is for anyone who is tired of living in survival mode.

Before you reach for anger.

Before you reach for pills.

Before you reach for regret.

Reach for your breath.

And watch your life change - one inhale at a time.

Kicking Depression in the Butt
is a raw, faith-infused, and deeply practical guide for anyone who is tired of surviving in silence and ready to reclaim their life.

Drawing from her own lived experiences with trauma, abandonment, loss, and depression, SaBrina Fisher Reece invites readers into an honest conversation about what depression really feels like,and how to fight back. This book does not minimize pain or offer shallow positivity. Instead, it helps readers recognize depression as an internal enemy, interrupt destructive thought cycles, and rebuild their inner world with intention, truth, and daily tools that actually work.

Through personal storytelling, spiritual insight, and mindset-shifting strategies, SaBrina shows readers how to stop identifying with their darkest thoughts and begin designing a life that protects their peace. She addresses the realities of trauma, triggers, boundaries, faith, therapy, medication, and personal responsibility, offering a balanced approach that honors both professional support and inner work.

Kicking Depression in the Butt is for the person who keeps showing up while quietly falling apart. It is for those who smile while suffering, who feel strong on the outside but exhausted on the inside. Most of all, it is a reminder that depression may visit, but it does not get to stay, and it does not get to become your identity.

This book is not about perfection. It's about progress. It's about learning how to fight for your mind, your peace, and your future, one thought, one choice, and one day at a time.

Because as long as you have breath in your body, your story is not over, and you still have the power to kick depression in the butt.

www.ingramcontent.com/pod-product-compliance
Lightning Source LLC
LaVergne TN
LVHW010837120826
845149LV00017B/1480